Vocation

The Lutheran Difference Series

Angus Menuge

CONCORDIA PUBLISHING HOUSE • SAINT LOUIS

Copyright © 2006 by Concordia Publishing House
3558 S. Jefferson Ave., St. Louis, MO 63118-3968
1-800-325-3040 • www.cph.org

All rights reserved. No part of this publication may be reproduced, stored in a retrieval system, or transmitted, in any form or by any means, electronic, mechanical, photocopying, recording, or otherwise, without the prior written permission of Concordia Publishing House.

Written by Angus Menuge

Edited by Robert C. Baker

Scripture quotations are from The Holy Bible, English Standard Version. Copyright © 2001 by Crossway Bibles, a publishing ministry of Good News Publishers, Wheaton, Illinois. Used by permission. All rights reserved.

The quotations from the Lutheran Confessions in this publication are from *Concordia: The Lutheran Confessions*, second edition, copyright © 2006 Concordia Publishing House. All rights reserved.

This publication may be available in braille, in large print, or on cassette tape for the visually impaired. Please allow 8 to 12 weeks for delivery. Write to Lutheran Blind Mission, 7550 Watson Rd., St. Louis, MO 63119-4409; call toll-free 1-888-215-2455; or visit the Web site: www.blindmission.org.

Manufactured in the United States of America

1 2 3 4 5 6 7 8 9 10   15 14 13 12 11 10 09 08 07 06

Contents

About This Series 4
Student Introduction 5
An Overview of Christian Denominations 6
Lutheran Facts 9
    Called to be Christ's 10
    Redeemed into Service 14
    Ruler of the Realms 18
    Ordered by Design 22
    The Great Dance 26
    God at Work 30
Leader Guide Introduction 34
    Answers 35
Appendix of Lutheran Teaching 59
Glossary 62

> **Hymnal Key**
> *LSB=Lutheran Service Book*
> *LW=Lutheran Worship*

About This Series

"It's just a job. I can leave any time that I want."
"Well, it's more than a job."
"What do you mean?"
"It's your *vocation*. God has given you gifts to serve others."

As Lutherans interact with other Christians, they often find themselves struggling to explain their beliefs and practices. Although many Lutherans have learned the "what" of the doctrines of the church, they do not always have a full scriptural foundation to share the "why." When confronted with different doctrines, they cannot clearly state their faith, much less understand the differences.

Because of insecurities about explaining particular doctrines or practices, some Lutherans may avoid opportunities to share what they have learned from Christ and His Word. The Lutheran Difference Bible study series will identify how Lutherans differ from other Christians and show from the Bible why Lutherans differ. These studies will prepare Lutherans to share their faith and help non-Lutherans understand the Lutheran difference.

Student Introduction

Today, Christians are pressed from every side to limit the role of faith in their life. A politician can have Christian convictions so long as they are not related to his or her public office. Christians can express their faith in worship, but often see little connection between faith and their work life. Not only secularists, but also some Christians, believe that faith should be truncated in this way. We often hear the mantra, "My faith is one thing, my profession another." Indeed, some Christians do integrate faith and work in quite inappropriate ways. A Christian auto mechanic who leaves evangelistic tracts in each car but fails to repair them is not a good Christian witness.

What is missing from the discussion is an understanding of *vocation*, or calling. Lutherans are aware that clergy and other church workers are not simply hired but are *called* by God through the congregation. Catechized Lutherans are also aware of a wider sense in which all Christians are servants: the priesthood of all believers. This is often taken to mean only that each Christian is called to spread the Gospel and to lead an ethical life. But there is much more to it than that. God provides each Christian layperson with gifts and circumstances that define a *station* in life. The purpose of this station is to serve our neighbors, to play a part in God's providential care of humanity. This means that even the work with low worldly status is something God calls us to do.

In our age, intense spiritual experience is exalted as the sign of God's favor. Ordinary work is often seen as a spiritually dead, practical necessity. But God did not save humankind with spectacular displays of power but through the crucifixion of Jesus. God does not call us to revel in private spiritual gifts, but to take up our crosses and to do His work. It is here that we find what Gene Edward Veith calls the "spirituality of ordinary life." The life-changing implications of this perspective are the focus of our Bible study.

An Overview of Christian Denominations

The following outline of Christian history will help you understand where the different denominations come from and how they are related to one another. Use this outline in connection with the "Comparisons" sections found throughout the study. Statements of belief for the different churches were drawn from their official confessional writings.

The Great Schism

Eastern Orthodox: On July 16, 1054, Cardinal Humbert entered the Cathedral of the Holy Wisdom in Constantinople just before the worship service. He stepped to the altar and left a letter condemning Michael Cerularius, patriarch of Constantinople. Cerularius responded by condemning the letter and its authors. In that moment, Christian churches of the east and west were severed from one another. Their disagreements centered on what bread could be used in the Lord's Supper and the addition of the *filioque* statement to the Nicene Creed.

The Reformation

Lutheran: On June 15, 1520, Pope Leo X wrote a letter condemning Dr. Martin Luther for his Ninety-five Theses. Luther's theses had challenged the sale of indulgences, a fund-raising effort to pay for the building of St. Peter's Cathedral in Rome. The letter charged Luther with heresy and threatened to excommunicate him if he did not retract his writings within sixty days. Luther replied by publicly burning the letter. Leo excommunicated him on January 3 and condemned all who agreed with Luther or supported his cause.

Reformed: In 1522, the preaching of Ulrich Zwingli in Zurich, Switzerland convinced people to break their traditional Lenten fast. Also, Zwingli preached that priests should be allowed to marry. When local friars challenged these departures from medieval church practice, the Zurich Council supported Zwingli and agreed that the

Bible should guide Christian doctrine and practice. Churches of this Reformed tradition include Presbyterians and Episcopalians.

Anabaptist: In January 1525, Conrad Grebel, a follower of Ulrich Zwingli, rebaptized Georg Blaurock. Blaurock began rebaptizing others and founded the Swiss Brethren. Their insistence on adult, believers' Baptism distinguished them from other churches of the Reformation. Anabaptists attracted social extremists who advocated violence in the cause of Christ, complete pacifism, or communal living. Mennonites, Brethren, and Amish churches descend from this movement.

The Counter Reformation

Roman Catholic: When people call the medieval church "Roman Catholic," they make a common historical mistake. Roman Catholicism emerged after the Reformation. As early as 1518, Luther and other reformers had appealed to the Pope and requested a council to settle the issue of indulgences. Their requests were hindered or denied for a variety of theological and political reasons. Finally, on December 13, 1545, thirty-four leaders from the churches who opposed the Reformation gathered at the invitation of Pope Paul III. They began the Council of Trent (1545–1563), which established the doctrine and practice of Roman Catholicism.

Post-Reformation Movements

Baptist: In 1608 or 1609, John Smyth, a former pastor of the Church of England, baptized himself by pouring water over his head. He formed a congregation of English Separatists in Holland, who opposed the rule of bishops and infant baptism. This marked the start of the English Baptist churches, which remain divided doctrinally over the theology of John Calvin (Particular Baptists) and Jacob Arminius (General Baptists). In the 1800s, the Restoration Movement of Alexander Campbell, a former Presbyterian minister, adopted many Baptist teachings. These churches include the Disciples of Christ (Christian Churches) and the Churches of Christ.

Wesleyan: In 1729, John and Charles Wesley gathered with three other men to study the Scriptures, receive communion, and discipline one another according to the "method" laid down in the Bible. Later, John Wesley's preaching caused religious revivals in England and America. Methodists, Wesleyans, Nazarenes, and Pentecostals form the Wesleyan family of churches.

Liberal: In 1799, Friedrich Schleiermacher published *Addresses on Religion* in an attempt to make Christianity appealing to people influenced by rationalism. He argued that religion is not a body of doctrines, provable truths, or a system of ethics but belongs to the realm of feelings. His ideas did not form a new denomination but deeply influenced Christian thinking. Denominations most thoroughly affected by liberalism are the United Church of Christ, Disciples of Christ, and Unitarianism.

Lutheran Facts

All who worship the Holy Trinity and trust in Jesus Christ for the forgiveness of sins are regarded by Lutherans as fellow Christians, despite denominational differences.

Lutheran churches first described themselves as "evangelische" or evangelical churches. Opponents of these churches called them "Lutheran" after Dr. Martin Luther, the sixteenth-century German church reformer.

Lutherans are not disciples of Dr. Martin Luther but disciples of Jesus Christ. They proudly accept the name Lutheran because they agree with Dr. Luther's teaching from the Bible, as summarized in Luther's Small Catechism.

Late medieval Roman Catholic theology emphasized the holiness of religious vocations (clergy, members of various religious orders, etc.). In contrast, Luther emphasized the holiness of everyday life. Christian mothers caring for their children, Christian fathers working to support their families, Christian soldiers following orders and doing their duty—each of these are God-given vocations of service toward one's neighbor.

Lutheran Christians understand that vocation is exercised in relationships. Before God, Christians are alone in their relationship with God, a relationship in which *He* serves *them*. But with their neighbor they are in a relationship in which *God* serves their neighbor *through them*. Father, mother, son, and daughter are, according to one Lutheran theologian, "biological orders" in which God serves members of the family. Other spheres of service include our daily work as employees or employers, citizens, teachers, electricians, or volunteers. God even uses people without faith to serve others here on earth. However, only the work of Christians done in faith is truly a good work in God's eyes.

Although God's work of love through our vocations serves our neighbor, our service does not obtain the forgiveness of sins. Our full forgiveness was won by Christ through His spotless life, bitter sufferings and death, and glorious resurrection. The fulfilling of our vocations is merely the fruit of lives transformed by God's redeeming grace.

To prepare for "Called to Be Christ's," read Ephesians 2:4–10.

Called to be Christ's

I fled Him, down the nights and down the days;
I fled Him, down the arches of the years;
... But with unhurrying chase,
And unperturbèd pace,
... Came on the following Feet,
And a Voice above their beat—
... 'Whom wilt thou find to love ignoble thee
Save Me, save only Me?
... Rise, clasp My hand, and come!'

—Francis Thompson, *The Hound of Heaven*

Since the fall into sin, all humans are by nature enemies of God. There is a huge chasm between a holy God and sinful humanity. Humans have no power to change the situation: we are not only lost, but incapable of reorienting ourselves. However, our God is a gracious God, a good shepherd who seeks out His lost sheep. He sent His only Son to lead the perfect life and to atone for our inability to do so, by suffering and dying on a cross. God shows that Jesus' sacrifice is complete by raising Him bodily from the dead. But there is more. Our sinful nature must also be put to death so that we find new life in Christ. God does this by uniting us in Holy Baptism with Christ's death and resurrection, calling us out of the darkness of sin to the light of Christ.

1. Have you ever found yourself in a difficulty where there was *nothing* you could do to repair the situation, but someone else was able to help? How did that experience change you? What insight can it give us into God's love for us?

Lost and Found

2. Read Psalm 51:1–12 and Romans 8:5–8. Why is it that human beings cannot make themselves acceptable to God? Why should Christians be skeptical of self-help religion?

3. Continue reading Romans 8:9–17. Also read the parable of the prodigal son (Luke 15:11–32). What does the Spirit of Christ do to transform an enemy of God into a child of God?

4. Read Titus 3:5–8 and Romans 6:1–14. What means does God use to connect us to the salvation won for us by Christ? What is the connection between the Christian and Christ?

5. Read Matthew 28:19–20. How important is Baptism for Jesus? What is the significance of the fact that Baptism requires water and the name of our triune God?

6. Read Genesis 1:28 and consider the fact that we are born of human parents. What important similarity is there between our physical existence and our new life in Christ?

A Royal Family

Being put right with God does not earn the world's favor. However, Christians are the adopted children of God Himself; we belong to the most royal family.

7. Read 1 Peter 2:9–10 and Romans 8:28–30. What is special about the family and household of God? How does election show God's special care for every one of us?

8. Read 1 Timothy 2:3–4 and Ephesians 1:3–14. Does election mean that non-Christians we know are without hope and are not loved by God? What do we learn from Ephesians 1:13?

Gifted and Talented

God does not *save* us to *shelve* us. God has work for us to do, and He knows that workers need the right tools for the job. We have natural gifts, but also need spiritual ones to see and do His will.

9. Read Ephesians 2:8–10 and 6:10–18. How does God equip us when He calls us? What are some of His specific gifts?

10. Read 1 Corinthians 2:6–16 and Romans 12:2. What is the practical connection between spiritual gifts and God's will?

Comparisons

Eastern Orthodox: "What is necessary in order to please God and to save one's own soul? In the first place, a knowledge of the true God, and a right faith in Him; in the second place, a life according to faith, and good works" (*The Longer Catechism of the Eastern Church*, Question 3).

Lutheran: "Our churches teach that people cannot be justified before God by their own strength, merits, or works. People are freely justified for Christ's sake, through faith, when they believe that they are received into favor and that their sins are forgiven for Christ's sake" (Augsburg Confession IV 1–2).

Reformed/Presbyterian: "Those whom God effectually calls, He also freely justifies; not by infusing righteousness into them, but by pardoning their sins . . . for Christ's sake alone" (*The Westminster Confession of Faith* XI:I).

Roman Catholic: "Whereas all men had lost their innocence in the prevarication of Adam . . . free will . . . was by no means extinguished in them" (*The Canons and Decrees of the Council of Trent*, Session 6, I).

Baptist: "We believe that the great gospel blessing which Christ secures to such as believe in him is Justification; that Justification includes the pardon of sin, and the promise of eternal life on principles of righteousness; that it is bestowed . . . solely through faith in the Redeemer's blood" (*The New Hampshire Baptist Confession* V).

Wesleyan/Methodist: "We are accounted righteous before God only for the merit of our Lord and Saviour Jesus Christ, by faith, and not for our own works or deservings" (*Methodist Articles of Religion* IX).

Liberal: "The traditional soteriology presupposed the historicity of Adam's fall and started from the assumption that mankind needs to be saved primarily from the taint inherited from Adam. But modern anthropology has discredited this way of determining the nature of man and of sin" (Gerald Birney Smith in *A Guide to the Study of the Christian Religion*, p. 519).

Point to Remember

Now if we have died with Christ, we believe that we will also live with Him. Romans 6:8

To prepare for "Redeemed into Service," read 1 Corinthians 12:4–6.

Redeemed into Service

> *Yet take thy way; for sure thy way is best:*
> *Stretch or contract me, thy poore debter:*
> *This is but tuning of my breast,*
> *To make the musick better.*

—George Herbert, *The Temper*

Modern consumer society panders to our preferences. This tempts us to suppose that service to God is simply a matter of choice. But when it comes to our relationship with God, God always chooses us. He creates us, elects us, redeems us, and brings us to saving faith. We were redeemed at a price—the ransom Jesus paid for us on the cross. But we are redeemed for a purpose. The natural and spiritual gifts that God provides us are to be used to serve our neighbor, attending to his or her physical and spiritual needs.

The calling to serve others is not a mystery of faith, but a concrete reality defined by our specific gifts and circumstances. Someone with the gift of teaching among those who need to learn has already been given a vocation. We may reject our calling, or embrace it but perform it badly, but the calling remains as an objective reality all the same. Calls change people; they are crosses that crucify our sinful egoism. Through Christ's suffering and death upon the cross, we are brought new life, and become servants who follow Christ by putting the needs of others before our own.

11. Recall a time when you were required to go somewhere you really did not want to go, but then found meaning and even joy in the opportunity to serve. What does this tell you about human nature, and how does it relate to God's plan for us in vocation?

God's Eyes and Hands

12. Read 1 Corinthians 7:17–24 and Luke 10:29–37. Does God call us away from our current station in life? In the most practical sense, who is the neighbor we are called to serve?

13. Read Luke 19:11–27. How does God view those who neglect their talents? What kind of result does He expect?

14. Read Romans 12:3–8. Why does God give different gifts to different Christians? Is He being arbitrary or unfair or does He have a better reason?

15. Read 1 Corinthians 12:12–26. How are the various gifts related to one another? Are all gifts important or are some merely consolation prizes?

16. Read Ephesians 4:1–6. Are the differences in gifts reason for jealousy and discord or is there a higher purpose?

Loving Our Neighbor

When God commands us to love our neighbor He is not calling for a warm fuzzy feeling, but a life of self-sacrificial service. God calls us to love our neighbor through the vocations He sends to us.

17. Read Romans 13:9–10 and 1 Corinthians 13. What is the connection between love and God's Law? What is true love like?

18. Read 1 John 3:11–20. What is the connection between God's love and a Christian's actions of love? What is the importance of self-sacrifice?

No Longer Aliens

Every vocation involves a relationship. Sin breaks relationships, making us aliens to God, our neighbor, and even to ourselves. But the new life in Christ received through faith restores these relationships, making us friends and loyal subjects.

19. Read Romans 12:9–21. How can God's love in Christ overcome the conflicts that undermine our relationships?

20. Read 2 Corinthians 5:11–21. How does God change us to restore our relationships? What is our model for reconciliation?

Comparisons

Eastern Orthodox: "How have we salvation by Christ's doctrine? When we receive it with all our heart, and walk according to it" (*The Longer Catechism of the Eastern Church*, Question 197).
Lutheran: "Our churches teach that that this faith is bound to bring forth good fruit (Galatians 5:22–23). It is necessary to do good works commanded by God (Ephesians 2:10), because of God's will. We should not rely on those works to merit justification before God.

The forgiveness of sins and justification is received through faith" (Augsburg Confession VI 1–2).

Reformed/Presbyterian: "They who are once effectually called, and regenerated, . . . are further sanctified . . . by His Word and Spirit dwelling in them" (*The Westminster Confession of Faith* XIII:I).

Roman Catholic: "Having, therefore, been thus justified . . . through the observance of the commandments of God and of the Church, faith co-operating with good works, [they] increase in that justice . . . and are still further justified" (*The Canons and Decrees of the Council of Trent,* Session 6, X).

Baptist: "We believe that Sanctification is the process by which, according to the will of God, we are made partakers of His holiness" (*The New Hampshire Baptist Confession* X).

Wesleyan/Methodist: "Good works . . . are . . . pleasing and acceptable to God in Christ, and spring out of a true and lively faith" (*Methodist Articles of Religion* X).

Liberal: "We cannot define Christian ethics in terms of a church-controlled society. Neither can we regard Christian duty as identical with biblical precepts . . ." (Gerald Birney Smith in *A Guide to the Study of the Christian Religion*, p. 570).

Point to Remember

Beloved, if God so loved us, we also ought to love one another. 1 John 4:11

To prepare for "Ruler of the Realms," read Matthew 22:15–22.

Ruler of the Realms

Now is the time for all good men to come to the aid of their country.
—Manual typewriting exercise

Our God governs us through two kingdoms or realms. In the kingdom of the left (civil government), God governs us through human authorities, such as parents, the legal system, and our political leaders. In the kingdom of the right (the Church), God governs believers through the Gospel in Word and Sacrament. Although saved by grace, Christians belong to both realms. In this life, we are simultaneously saints and sinners.

Most of the time, our obligation to earthly authorities is clear. However, these authorities are under God's Law, and when an officeholder requires us to do something against God's Law, the Christian must serve God rather than men. A human judgment that contradicts God's Law is not valid, for although there are two kingdoms, there is only one King, God.

21. Consider someone who claims to be Christian but rejects the state's authority because the only boss they recognize is the "Jewish carpenter." Is their rejection of human authority justified? Are they missing something important? When a Christian nurse is required to participate in a legal abortion procedure, he or she discovers a conflict between human law and God's Word. Whose authority should prevail?

Under His Authority

22. Read Matthew 3:13–17 and 26:39–42. How does Jesus' own life reveal acceptance of God the Father's authority?

23. Read Philippians 2:1–11. What is the connection between Christ's humility and our own?

24. Read Romans 13. Do Christians need to respect man-made rules? Does an earthly ruler derive authority from the power of his military or the number of votes she received?

25. Read Acts 5:27–32. Under what conditions are Christians called to practice civil disobedience? What if a totalitarian or Islamic state makes evangelism illegal?

26. Read Ephesians 6:5–9 and 1 Corinthians 7:21–23. What is the Christian response to an oppressive vocation, like slavery or work for unfair pay, for unreasonable hours, or in unsafe conditions?

Family Matters

In the Large Catechism, Luther tells us that parents are the pre-eminent representatives of God's authority on earth. Children who reject their parents' authority typically reject every other authority as well, and become dysfunctional citizens and poor employees. Rejection of God's representatives is rejection of God's authority, and flows from unbelief.

By contrast, children who humbly accept the authority of their parents learn to accept God's representatives in society and the Church. They become valued citizens and workers and are more likely to remain faithful members of a church.

27. Read Deuteronomy 5:16 and Ephesians 6:1–4. What connection does family have to the wider community?

28. Read Acts 16:29–34. What connection is suggested between a human family and the family of faith?

Church and State

Church and State have different vocations. The State does not save, nor is the Church called to maintain law and order. Yet Christians should support the State unless it violates God's Law or impedes the Gospel.

29. Read John 18:33–37; 19:11; and Psalm 146:3–6. What is the practical difference between the kingdom of grace and the kingdom of this world?

30. Read John 17:14–18 and Romans 12:1–2. Does Jesus call us out of the world? Does serving our neighbor mean being worldly?

Comparisons

Lutheran: "Our teachers' position is this: the authority of the Keys (Matthew 16:19), or the authority of bishops—according to the Gospel—is a power or commandment of God, to preach the Gospel, to forgive and retain sins, and to administer the Sacraments. . . . For civil government deals with other things than the Gospel does. Civil rulers do not defend minds, but bodies and bodily things against obvious injuries. They restrain people with the sword and physical punishment in order to preserve civil justice and peace (Romans 13:1–7). Therefore, the Church's authority and the State's authority must not be confused" (Augsburg Confession, Article XXVIII 5, 11–12, 1530).

Reformed: "The civil magistrate may not assume to himself the administration of the Word and Sacraments, or the power of the keys of the kingdom of heaven: yet he hath authority, and it is his duty to take order that unity and peace be preserved in the Church, that the truth of God be kept pure and entire, that all blasphemies and heresies be suppressed, all corruptions and abuses in worship and discipline prevented or reformed, and all the ordinances of God duly settled, administered, and observed. For the better effecting whereof he hath power to call synods, to be present at them, and to provide that whatsoever is transacted in them be according to the mind of God" (*The Westminster Confession of Faith* XXIII 3, 1647; the American revision to this confession was adapted to the separation of Church and State.).

Roman Catholic: [The following points are rejected; the opposite points are considered true.] "54. Kings and princes are not only exempt from the jurisdiction of the Church, but are superior to the Church, in litigated questions of jurisdiction. . . . 55. The Church ought to be separated from the State, and the State from the Church" (*The Papal Syllabus of Errors*, section 7, decreed by Pope Pius IX, December 8, 1864; individual condemnations are considered infallible by some Roman Catholic theologians.).

Point to Remember

Obey your leaders and submit to them, for they are keeping watch over your souls, as those who will have to give an account. Hebrews 13:17

To prepare for "Ordered by Design," read Matthew 19:3–6.

Ordered by Design

Turning and turning in the widening gyre
The falcon cannot hear the falconer;
Things fall apart; the centre cannot hold;
Mere anarchy is loosed upon the world.
—W.B. Yeats, *The Second Coming*

Modern secular society emphasizes equality and democracy. In many ways this is good. Everyone is equally valuable to God, and everyone should have a voice in how government is run. But that does not mean that vocations are interchangeable. And the right to voice an opinion does not make all opinions equally authoritative.

God created order out of chaos. This order is reflected in distinctions in vocation. Not every living thing has the same purpose. Only humans are called to be stewards over creation. Men and women are not interchangeable units in an androgynous society. Husband is a different vocation from wife. Father is a different vocation from mother. The fact that vocations have equal importance does not imply that no one has to submit to anyone else. Children are as important as parents but must submit to their parents' authority. Wives are as important as husbands, but must submit to their husbands' authority. Parents, however, must not embitter, but serve their children. Husbands are called to love their wives in self-sacrifice as Christ loves the Church.

31. Why do people resist order in groups? Have you ever encountered a group in which a bossy person usurped someone else's job? What damage did it do to the group? Does God have a better idea for how to live together?

Made to Order

32. Read Genesis 1:26–28. What is special about the design of human beings? What special task is given to them alone in all of creation?

33. Read Genesis 2:15–24. How does this passage show that male/female distinctions are part of God's *original* design and not simply the consequence of the fall, as some have argued?

34. Read Genesis 3:14–19. What curses are laid upon the vocations of men and women as a consequence of the fall? What is the promise in verse 15?

35. Read Romans 5:12–21 and Ephesians 2:1–10. How did Christ deal with Adam's sin and its consequences? How does this restore and motivate our vocations?

36. Read Ephesians 5:21–33 and 1 Peter 3:1–8. What is God's design for marriage? Do these passages only call women to make sacrifices?

Order in Society

In *King Lear*, Shakespeare shows how family breakdown leads to the decline of civilization. Our vocations call us to maintain God's order in family and society by respecting God's design for humanity.

37. Read Judges 21:25 and 2 Timothy 3:1–5. What happens to society when people reject authority? Relate to contemporary examples.

38. Read 1 Peter 4:1–11. What can Christians contribute to social order today?

Order in the Church

Today we suffer from vocational confusion in the Church. Laity sometimes usurp pastoral work. Pastors take on work better handled by qualified laity. Many want more "exciting" worship. Some women "feel" called to be a pastor. All of this distracts from the life of humble, selfless service that Christ calls for.

39. Read 1 Corinthians 14:26–40. How are we called to worship?

40. Read 1 Timothy 2:8–15. How should we understand the role of women in the Church?

For Reflection

Christ's endorsement of matrimony is supported throughout the Scriptures. When the prophets of the Old Covenant sought to impress upon their own countrymen the magnificence of [God's] grace to Israel and the mystic union that bound Him to His people, they could find no more fitting symbol than marriage, the intimate union that exists between husband and wife. Long into the New Testament the same exaltation of marriage continues. Writing to the Ephesians (5:25) and consciously speaking of a great mystery, St. Paul compares the love which a husband bears for his wife to that self-effacing devotion with which Jesus loved the Church. And as the light of revelation illumines the closing pages of St. John's Apocalypse, the bride, the holy Church, gazes along the horizon of prophecy for the coming of the Bridegroom, Christ.

Walter A. Maier, *For Better Not for Worse* (Concordia Publishing House, 1939), p. 75.

Point to Remember

He is before all things, and in Him all things hold together. Colossians 1:17

To prepare for "The Great Dance," read Ephesians 4:11–16.

The Great Dance

*O chestnut-tree, great-rooted blossomer
Are you the leaf, the blossom or the bole?
O body swayed to music, O brightening glance,
How can we know the dancer from the dance?*

—W. B. Yeats, *Among School Children*

Our triune God shows diversity, order, and relationship within His own being. Although the Son is coequal with the Father, the Son chooses the way of obedience, humbling Himself to become man and dying on a cross for our sins. Then the dance changes and the Son is exalted to the right hand of the Father. The Holy Spirit is also an active participant with a special role. He proceeds from the Father and the Son, convicting the world of sin, calling people to faith and making them holy.

There is another dance, the great dance of marriage, where man and woman become one flesh, living in reverence for Christ. The dance widens to family and then community. Each person has many roles in the dance. Men and women are born into the vocation of son and daughter, and may later find themselves husband and wife, father and mother, worker, volunteer, and member of a congregation.

41. Recall a sports game or a meeting where a few people wanted to do all of the work. What happened? What can we learn from this about vocation?

A Play with Many Parts

42. Read Luke 3:12–14. Why is it important that John the Baptist's call to repentance does not require abandoning worldly vocations?

43. Re-read Romans 12:4–8. Why are there so many different vocations?

44. Re-read 1 Corinthians 12:14–26. In God's eyes are any vocations unimportant? How are different vocations connected?

45. Read 1 Thessalonians 4:1–12. How does Paul's advice contribute to the great dance of community?

46. Read 2 Thessalonians 3:6–10. What does Paul say about those who would prefer to sit out the dance?

47. Read 2 Thessalonians 3:11–13. What is the difference between being busy and being a busybody? What impact does each have on the great dance?

Wearing Many Hats

The same person can have many callings at the same time. A Christian businessman is simultaneously called to be a Christian, a church member, a husband and father, and a salesman. The callings affect one another in important ways. For example, a Christian businessman should not allow his work to undermine his familial roles and should see his work as a means of supporting his family and of witness. Additionally, he should conduct his business in a fair and honest manner, his actions reflecting his beliefs positively to unbelievers.

48. Read 1 Timothy 3:1–13. How does this show that we hold many vocations simultaneously *and* that they are interconnected? Apply this to your own vocations.

49. Read Acts 26. How does Paul use his multiplicity of vocations to be a more effective witness for Christ? What can we learn about our daily callings and our opportunities for witness?

A Road Less Traveled

Some of the best things that happen to us are not our idea. Changes in circumstance or relationships can be painful, yet also provide new opportunities for service.

50. Read Genesis 50:15–21. How does Joseph's story show that God can even work through human evil to provide an important calling?

51. Read Exodus 6:28–7:7 and Acts 9:1–16. How do the examples of Moses and Paul illustrate how God calls us out of our "comfort zone"?

Comparisons

Eastern Orthodox: "Is the Holy Ghost communicated to men even now likewise? He is communicated to all true Christians. . . . How may we be made partakers of the Holy Ghost? Through fervent prayer, and through the Sacraments" (*Longer Catechism of the Eastern Church*, Questions 249–250).

Lutheran: "I believe that I cannot by my own reason or strength believe in Jesus Christ, my Lord, or come to Him; but the Holy Spirit has called me by the Gospel, enlightened me with His gifts, sanctified and kept me in the true faith" (Luther's Small Catechism, "The Creed," Third Article). Lutherans emphasize that the Holy Spirit works through the means of grace: the Word and Sacraments.

Reformed: "But when God accomplishes His good pleasure in the elect, or works in them true conversion, He not only causes the gospel to be externally preached to them, and powerfully illuminates their minds by His Holy Spirit . . . but by the efficacy of the same regenerating Spirit He pervades the inmost recesses of the man" (*Canons of the Synod of Dort*, Art. XI).

Roman Catholic: The Holy Spirit awakens faith in unbelievers and communicates new life to them through the ministry of the Church.

Anabaptist: This movement emphasizes the mystical work of the Spirit in the heart rather than through Word and Sacraments. Only holy people have received the Holy Spirit and are members of the church.

Baptist: "We believe that Repentance and Faith are sacred duties, and also inseparable graces, wrought in our souls by the regenerating Spirit of God" (*New Hampshire Baptist Confession* VIII).

Wesleyan: "But as soon as he is born of God . . . he is now capable of hearing the inward voice of God, saying, 'Be of good cheer; thy sins are forgiven thee'; 'Go and sin no more.' . . . He 'feels in his heart,' to use the language of our Church, 'the mighty working of the Spirit of God'" (*Standard Sermons of John Wesley*, 45.II.4).

Point to Remember

If one member suffers, all suffer together; if one part is honored, every part rejoices with it. 1 Corinthians 12:26

To prepare for "God at Work," read Matthew 20:25–28.

God at Work

In co-operation in vocation, man becomes God's mask on earth . . . God reveals himself to others through man's actions.

—Gustaf Wingren, *Luther on Vocation* (Muhlenberg Press, 1957)

Everything we have is God's. We are saved by grace and not by works. So God does not *need* any of our vocations. But our neighbor does. God calls us into vocations to serve our neighbor, not to save or serve ourselves. But vocations are not merely human works. God works through us.

As Luther explains, we are God's masks (*larvae Dei*): His eyes, hands and feet. Although God could provide everything directly, He chooses to work through human beings. Just as the Gospel is communicated through the means of grace (Word and Sacrament), so God's providential care for humanity is channeled through the means of vocations. To use Gene Edward Veith's example in *God at Work*, God could provide bread directly, as He did to Israel in the desert. But normally God provides through the vocations of farmer, truck driver, baker, and store clerk. Vocations are the channels of God's ongoing love for creation.

52. Have you ever found yourself doing something that helped someone else even though you had not planned on doing it? What can we learn about how God works?

Our Servant God

53. Read Matthew 6:27–34. What do we learn about our temporal needs, like clothing, drink, and food?

54. Read John 13:14–17 and re-read Philippians 2:1–11. How does Jesus lead us into a life of service?

55. Read Colossians 1:9–14 and Galatians 5:22–26. How does God work through us and what fruit does He produce?

56. Read 1 Corinthians 3:4–9. In what sense are man and God "fellow workers"?

57. Read Philippians 1:18–26. How does Paul show that God works even through our weaker efforts here on earth?

58. Read John 15:1–8 and Ephesians 2:19–22. How does God build the Christian community by working through us?

Mutual Dependence

In his book, *Civility*, Stephen Carter argues that we often fall prey to *individualism*, the idea that we are independent and completely in charge of our lives. But a great piano player needs a music teacher, the composers and printers of the music, the parent who took him to lessons, the automobile workers who built the car, the road workers who build and maintain the roads, and many others.

59. Re-read 1 Corinthians 12:21–26 and Ephesians 4:7–16. How does God's plan for us reject individualism?

60. Read Galatians 6:2–5. What can we learn from the fact that God calls us to carry our own load, yet also to bear each other's burdens?

Consider the Source

All pride and boasting comes from the tendency to take credit for the works of our own hands. But we are stewards, not landlords, of everything we have. Our very lives, bodies, and minds are gifts. So are our callings to serve others. God is love and transmits it like the light of the sun. At best we are like the moon. We are marred by the "craters" of sin and produce no light of our own. But by God's grace in Christ, we can reflect the light of God's love to others.

61. Read 1 John 4:7–21 and re-read Luke 10:19–37. Where does our love really come from? What answer can be given to the question, "Who is the good Samaritan?" How does this guide our life today?

62. Read James 1:17–18 and 2 Corinthians 9:6–15. What is the source and purpose of our gifts? Why does God value generosity? How can we apply this today?

Comparisons

The word *vocation* ("calling") is used in a variety of ways. The different uses of the word stem from different traditions in Western Christendom.

Medieval: The word *vocation* was used mainly to describe God's calling of servants in the Church. A *clerical vocation* meant a parish pastor. A *religious vocation* meant a person who lived as a monk or nun in isolation from broader society. (*Vocation* could also describe the fixed states in which people labored in medieval society: serfs, lords, and so on.) A sharp contrast was made between those called to serve God in the Church and all other workers. This view of vocation was important for later Roman Catholicism.

Lutheran: Martin Luther applied the word *vocation* not just to clergy, but to all workers. He emphasized that God commanded, blessed, and worked through all types of legitimate labor. The heavenly Father called people to different types of work so that they might bless one another.

Calvinist: John Calvin largely accepted Luther's view of vocation but added that labor should lead to profit as a mark of God's blessing. Later, some Calvinists came to view profit as a mark of election to salvation.

Anabaptist: Menno Simons and Jacob Hutter were influenced by Luther's view on vocation, but they taught that Christians could not legitimately serve in government. They also emphasized communal sharing of profit.

Modern: Since the Enlightenment, the tendency has been to separate vocation from God's call to work. Christianity taught people to live in service to God and His goals. In contrast, modern movements have taught people to live their lives for personal goals, state goals, or collective social goals. Vocation has come to mean one's career with no reference to God's calling.

Point to Remember

And God is able to make all grace abound to you, so that having all sufficiency in all things at all times, you may abound in every good work. 2 Corinthians 9:8

Leader Guide

Leaders, please note the different abilities of your class members. Some will easily find the many passages listed in this study. Others will struggle to find even the "easy" passages. To help everyone participate, team up members of the class. For example, if a question asks you to look up several passages, assign one passage to one group, the second to another, and so on. Divide up the work! Let participants present the different answers they discover.

Each topic is divided into four easy-to-use sections.

Focus: key concepts that will be discovered.

Inform: guides the participants into Scripture to uncover truth concerning a doctrine.

Connect: enables participants to apply that which is learned in Scripture to their lives and provides them an opportunity to formulate and articulate a defense of a key doctrine.

Vision: provides participants with practical suggestions for extending the theme of the lesson out of the classroom and into the world.

Called to be Christ's

Objectives

By the power of the Holy Spirit working through God's Word, participants will (1) see clearly that sin separates us from God, (2) understand that we have no power to recover God's favor, and (3) rejoice that God Himself restores us and calls us into His family by Holy Baptism.

Opening Worship

Opening worship might begin with a responsive reading of the four questions and answers on Holy Baptism in the Small Catechism (*LSB* 325; *LW*, pp. 303–04), especially noting that we are baptized into Christ's death and resurrection (question 4) and are called to a life of daily repentance. As James readily and faithfully followed his call to serve Jesus, a good prayer would be the Collect of the Day for St. James the Elder (*LSB Altar Book*, p. 971; *LW*, p. 98). An apt hymn is "Baptized into Your Name Most Holy" (*LSB* 590; *LW* 224).

Focus

1. Read, or ask a participant to read, the first paragraph. Discuss the difference between problems we can fix and chronic conditions that only someone else can help with. (Some examples may be medical, financial, employment, or relationship issues that we realize are beyond our control.) Relate this to the fact that humans cannot save themselves from sin, and how this is a "schoolmaster unto salvation," by showing our need for a savior. Continue with the second paragraph. Ask "What two roles are played by Jesus' death and resurrection?" It should emerge that there is a distinction between the fact of justification (Christ's atonement for the sins of all people) and its effect on us (the believer's justification in Baptism).

Lost and Found (Inform)

Sin is not a problem like a leaky sink or a car that does not start. Such problems can be fixed by human reason and ingenuity. Sin is an illness beyond our capacity to fix. Fortunately, Christ Himself is our great physician, atoning for our sin and then offering healing and regeneration in the waters of Holy Baptism.

2. David tells us that we are sinful from conception, that sin is an inherited disease that corrupts our human nature. This original sin is the result of the fall, and means that human beings are condemned to hell without God's regeneration. "[S]ince the fall of Adam all men who are born according to the course of nature are conceived and born in sin. . . . [T]his inborn sickness and hereditary sin is truly sin and condemns to the eternal wrath of God all those who are not born again through Baptism and the Holy Spirit." (*Augsburg Confession*, Article II). As Paul explains, the sinful nature is hostile to God and cannot please Him. Self-help religions deny the harsh facts of original sin and pretend that we can do what only God can do through the Holy Spirit (see the commentary on the Third Article of the Creed in the Small Catechism).

3. Paul goes on to explain that, through the power of the Holy Spirit, we are no longer enemies of God, but rather, through Christ, we are "sons of God" (Romans 8:14), "children of God" (v. 16), and His "heirs" (v. 17). As heirs, we inherit Christ's merits and benefits. Because of Christ's perfect righteousness, our "Spirit is life" (v. 10) and he "who raised Christ Jesus from the dead will also give life to your mortal bodies" (v. 11). In the parable of the prodigal son (Luke 15:11–32), we see how we walked away from God in our sin. Through the Law, God calls us to repentance. But this cannot save us. Our God is like the prodigal son's father who saw him far off and "felt compassion" (v. 20). Our heavenly Father welcomes back His lost sons and daughters and gives them the full rights of heirs.

4. We are saved "by the washing of regeneration and renewal of the Holy Spirit . . . poured out on us richly through Jesus Christ our Savior" (Titus 3:5–6). God calls Christians to faith through certain "proper channels," the means of grace (Word and Sacrament). One of these is Baptism. As Paul explains, in Baptism our sinful nature is put to death and we are given a new life in Christ. In Baptism, the Holy Spirit connects us to Christ: we are baptized into Christ's death and resurrection.

5. In the Great Commission, Jesus commands Baptism for people of "all nations" (Matthew 28:19). He makes no qualifications about age, and it is clear that Baptism is completely passive. The power of Baptism has nothing to do with how educated a person is or how "ready" they feel. This, and the fact that Baptism reconnects the lost to Christ, shows the importance of infant Baptism. In Baptism, the physical element (water) has no magical power, but the water is connected to the Word (the

invocation of the name of our triune God), through which the Holy Spirit works to regenerate the lost.

6. Our God is a God of means, who institutes a proper way in which His calls to us are made. Although God could create us directly, He calls us into human existence through the means of our human parents. Since we now inherit a corrupted human nature, our merciful God has instituted other means to restore us and to incorporate us into His family. Baptism is the means of new birth God institutes to create the new life in Christ that our human existence cannot claim for itself.

A Royal Family (Connect)

7. Many people suffer from feelings of insignificance because they lack wealth, fame, or an exciting job. It is vital that all Christians see that God has given them the highest approval and status possible. By adopting us as His own sons and daughters, God has incorporated us into the royal family of the King of the universe! Paul explains that this was all according to His plan, since God has always known each individual that He would save. As Christians, we can never say that God has forgotten about us or has faulty records. You might note the analogy provided by C. S. Lewis's *The Lion, the Witch and the Wardrobe*, in which four ordinary, secular children, Edmund, Peter, Lucy, and Susan are called to be kings and queens of Narnia.

8. It is God alone who saves. We must not assume that someone who claims to reject Christ by words or deeds cannot be saved (Consider the example of Paul.). We know that God wants all people to be saved and that He can work through even our halting efforts to witness. In Ephesians 1:13, we see that those who had been outside of Christ's salvation were included when they "heard the word of truth, the gospel of . . . salvation." God can and does work through our proclamation of that word to bring people to faith, so all Christians are called to witness.

Gifted and Talented (Vision)

9. God does not only save us by grace, He also *gifts* us by grace to do His work. We are God's "workmanship, created in Christ Jesus for good works, which God prepared beforehand, that we should walk in them" (Ephesians 2:10). Notice that, as we are incorporated into Christ's royal family, we are given the gifts we need to do His work. (In *The Lion, the Witch and the Wardrobe*, Aslan provides Edmund, Peter, Susan, and Lucy each with distinctive gifts that define their distinctive callings.) The spiritual gifts of all Christians include many pieces of "armor": "the belt of truth," the "breastplate of righteousness," the "shield

of faith," the "helmet of salvation" and the "sword of the spirit" (Ephesians 6:14–17). You may want to discuss the contribution of these gifts to daily life. For example, having a grounding in God's truth gives Christians a solid place to stand, independent of the shifting sands of politics and philosophy. Having Christ's righteousness as a gift means that we do not need to depend on our own inadequate righteousness, which is like "a polluted garment" (Isaiah 64:6) before God.

10. Spiritual gifts are not merely powers to do things. They are given along with the Spirit immediately in and through Baptism. With the power of the Holy Spirit, the eyes of faith are opened to a realm of spiritual reality. We can see the truth of God's love amidst a world of suffering and evil. We are taught words of divine wisdom from above that human reason can never reach up to or comprehend. We find the divine truth that God saves and renews us through grace, even though the truths of the Gospel remain "folly" to the non-Christian, who cannot "understand them because they are spiritually discerned" (1 Corinthians 2:14). And we also discern God's will for our life. This includes the ability to recognize our vocation. No longer are we bound to conform to the patterns of this world: our mind is renewed so that we can believe and live differently from those who find their home in this world. We have a citizenship from heaven and live here as resident aliens.

Discuss some specific ways in which Christians see the purpose of their lives differently than non-Christians. Examples could include: putting less store in accumulating possessions, doing work as a service to others and not merely for reward, and seeing that work as an opportunity to witness to coworkers and clients.

Redeemed into Service

Objectives

By the power of the Holy Spirit working through God's Word, participants will (1) see that God, not we, chooses our vocation, (2) understand that God calls us into service by our gifts and circumstances, and (3) realize that the purpose of vocation is loving our neighbor.

Opening Worship

Opening worship could focus on Hebrews 12:1–3, which keeps our eyes fixed on our redeemer, Jesus, and Hebrews 13:20–21, which emphasizes that God provides us with gifts to do His will. A good prayer would be the Collect of the Day for the Day of Special or National Thanksgiving (*LSB Altar Book*, p. 990 or 991; *LW*, p. 122). An apt hymn is "Lord of Glory, You Have Bought Us" (*LSB* 851; *LW* 402).

Focus

11. Review the last section ("Gifted and Talented") of the first study, and ask "Why does God provide gifts, whether natural or spiritual?" God is not just being nice but is enabling us to do the work He wants us to do. Read the two paragraphs and discuss the difference between paths we choose and paths that God chooses us for us. Ask, "Why is it so difficult for people today to see how God works?" We are used to seeing everything as our choice, and the idea of someone else choosing us and our path in life is alien and even threatening to our autonomy. Discuss how meaning can be found when we humble ourselves to God's will for our lives even when we do not want to do so. Human nature resists God's will, but God changes us through vocation so that, to our surprise, we find fulfillment in serving others.

God's Eyes and Hands (Inform)

12. God does not call us out of our circumstances into a special kind of holy, Christian living. Unless our activities are inherently sinful, God expects us to remain at our station. It is here, and with the gifts that

God has provided, that we are called to serve our neighbor. If we can avoid degrading or difficult work, we may do so, but even the worst work is an opportunity to serve and witness. The suffering slave may change the slaveowner's heart. In practice, our neighbor is always the person we encounter where we are, whether we like the person or not. The Good Samaritan found the robbery victim and had the gifts to help him. His calling was perfectly clear, defined by his circumstances and abilities, not some mystery requiring deep contemplation.

13. God's talents are an investment. An investor expects some return on his investment. When God "plants" us with gifts, He expects growth and fruit. When we discern our gifts, we simultaneously discern a call to use them. The more we are given, the more that is expected of us. Neglecting our talents is a sinful rejection of God's will and purpose for our life. But our God is a gracious God, and when we neglect or abuse our talents He calls us to repentance and a renewed life of service, graciously forgiving us of our sins.

14. It can seem unfair that God gives different gifts to different people, and that some of these gifts are considered better than others. But we must remember two things. First, we are entitled to none of these gifts and should therefore be thankful for those we do have. Second, God's purpose is for us to live in a community, in the body of Christ. A community cannot work if everyone does the same kind of work (e.g., everyone is a lawyer or tax collector) or if some kinds of work are neglected (no one collects the garbage or keeps hospitals clean). Likewise, an effective body cannot be made by many parts with the same function (e.g., many eyes). God wants us to discern our contribution to the proper functioning of civil society and the Church.

15. Paul goes on to explain that each part of the body of Christ needs the other parts: "The eye cannot say to the hand 'I have no need of you'" (1 Corinthians 12:21). The world makes all sorts of distinctions between different types of work in terms of pay and status, and some conclude that their work is unimportant. But the fact is that just as each part of the body is indispensable to the proper functioning of the body, so each vocation is indispensable to the body of Christ and to society. No vocations are more important than others. All are God-pleasing means of serving our neighbor.

16. When we think too closely about how our role compares with others, we sometimes lose sight of how all of these roles combine to fulfill God's intentions for community. We must remember that in the body of Christ our responsibility is to live a life "worthy of the calling to which" we "have been called" (Ephesians 4:1), that we are required to have "humility" and "patience, bearing with one another in love" (v. 2).

We are also called to unity in the Spirit. Jealousy and discord are enemies of this unity, and we should remind ourselves that, though we have different gifts, "there is one body and Spirit" and we are called to one hope, founded in "one Lord, one faith," and "one baptism" (v. 4–5).

Loving Our Neighbor (Connect)

17. God calls us to love our neighbor through our vocation. Although a pleasant disposition can be a good witness, this call does not simply mean being a nice, polite person on the job. True love is fulfillment of God's Law, and requires us to love our neighbor as ourselves (Romans 13:9–10). This love is "patient and kind" and avoids "envy" (1 Corinthians 13:4). "It does not insist on its own way" (v. 5) but puts the needs of our neighbor above our own. Our vocations are means of showing love for our neighbor by giving him or her what he or she really needs. This is accomplished by honest, trustworthy work of high quality, not by shoddy work adorned with superficial piety. As Luther reputedly said, the Christian cobbler should make good shoes, not poor shoes covered in crosses.

18. The pattern of true love is found in the cross of Christ. It is self-sacrificial love, love shown to others that seeks nothing in return. If need be, Christians are called to lay down their very life for others as Christ did for us. In our vocations, there is a sense in which we already do this, because we lay down the selfish cravings of our ego in order to serve others. In that sense, vocation, like Baptism, involves a kind of crucifixion and resurrection. We are not merely called to say the right words, to pay lip service to God's love, but to show our love "in deed and in truth" (1 John 3:18). Discuss specific examples of self-sacrificial lives. You might use a dramatic example like New York fire fighters charging back into the World Trade Center to save those trapped inside. But consider also how an ordinary plumber, carpenter, teacher, or businessman may kill his own desires to serve others.

No Longer Aliens (Vision)

19. Conflict arises from self-love, which makes us resent the accomplishments of others when we should be rejoicing in them. Self-sacrificial love makes us "love one another with brotherly affection" and honors others above ourselves (Romans 12:10). United with Christ in Baptism, we find in Him a source of joyful hope, patience, and faithful prayer (v. 12) that binds us together as a community and keeps us focused outward on those in need (v. 13). Unconditional love can love the persecutor (v. 14) and "associate with the lowly" (v. 16). The power of

this love is found in its lack of self-conscious pride, which causes us to take revenge and become angry at others because they harm us or thwart our preferences (vv. 17–20). True love can "overcome evil with good" (v. 21). Discuss a practical example where the showing of love to a wayward person eventually turned their life around. The person may be someone else the participant knows or the participant himself.

20. Relationships are destroyed when we choose to live for ourselves, neglecting our obligations to others. Christ restores relationships because He died for us all, so that we no longer live for ourselves but for Him (2 Corinthians 5:14–15). As a result, we should not look at other Christians "according to the flesh" (v. 16), but as a "new creation" (v. 17). Our God is not a "Do as I say, not as I do" kind of God. When God calls Christians to harmonious relationships, the foundation is God's own action of reconciliation. God "through Christ reconciled us to Himself and gave us the ministry of reconciliation" (v. 18). As God has reconciled us to Himself through Christ, we are called to be "ambassadors for Christ" (v. 20), creating new relationships by sharing this message of reconciliation with others. Discuss relationship problems and what helps people reconcile. For example, what happens when married couples find employment opportunities far from each other or disagree about having children? How are Christians called to handle these difficult decisions in ways that reflect God's reconciling, selfless love?

Ruler of the Realms

Objectives

By the power of the Holy Spirit working through God's Word, participants will (1) understand that there is one God, but He governs through two kingdoms or realms, (2) see that human authorities are instituted by God and Christians are bound to obey them unless those authorities require rejection of God's moral Law, and (3) realize that the family is the foundation for civil society and the Church.

Opening Worship

Opening worship could begin with reading together the Fourth Commandment and its explanation from the Small Catechism (*LSB* 321; *LW*, p. 300), supplemented with some commentary from the Large Catechism. A good prayer would be the Prayer for the Nation or Responsible Citizenship (*LSB* 313) or the Prayer for Good Government (*LW*, p. 126). An apt hymn is "Our Father, by Whose Name" (*LSB* 863; *LW* 465).

Focus

21. Read, or have a participant read, the first two paragraphs. Discuss why it is that Christians should obey man-made laws, such as those controlling speed limits, voter registration, and taxes. Consider the fact that if most people dissent from human laws, chaos arises and we cannot protect our own families or freely proclaim the Gospel. However, human laws cannot save and they remain subject to God's Law. If human laws obstruct the Gospel or contradict God's direct commands to a Christian, then those laws violate God's purpose and the Christian should be obedient to Christ's command. In the example given, the Christian nurse, even if it were to cost his or her job, should not participate in an abortion.

Under His Authority (Inform)

Humble obedience to authority is a crucial element of the Christian life. Christians are called to obey earthly authorities, starting with their parents, but also to reflect Christ's rule in their hearts by living lives of self-sacrificial love. The Christian is subject to both authorities in his or her vocation, where he or she must obey the law and do what his or her employer requires, yet also serve his or her neighbor in gratitude for what Christ has done for him or her.

22. Jesus models acceptance of authority, by humbling Himself to be baptized even though He was without sin. We learn from the Father's response (Matthew 3:17) that those who humble themselves to authority are exalted. Jesus' calling is to bear and atone for the sins of the world. Even with what lies before Him, Jesus humbly accepts His Father's will (Matthew 26:39). In our earthly vocations, we also are called to humbly accept God's will, seeing our neighbor as an opportunity for love, not an obstacle to self-fulfillment. When we follow this path, we discover a higher fulfillment in service well done than we could ever find in self-gratification. We must lose our lives to find them.

23. Paul develops this idea further. We see that the pattern of Christ's vocation is humiliation and exaltation (Philippians 2:6–11). This same pattern is laid out for our earthly vocations. We are called to be imitators of Christ's humility (vv. 1–5), which means accepting God's authority. Since this authority is manifest in two kingdoms or realms, we must live as humble citizens of both realms, obedient to earthly authority and to the fact that we are saved by God's grace through faith in Christ to serve others.

24. Tolstoy believed that all human laws violated the supremacy of Christ's rule in our heart, but he neglected the fact that Christ Himself said we should pay the taxes due to Caesar (Matthew 22:21). Paul explains that human authorities are established by God Himself (Romans 13:1) as means of maintaining order. You may want to comment on the first, or civil, use of the law, which serves as a curb against the worst consequences of outward sin. (Robert Bolt makes the point dramatically in his play *A Man For All Seasons*, in which Thomas More says that he would give the devil himself the benefit of law for his own safety's sake.) Paul clarifies that rebellion against human authority instituted by God is also rebellion against God (v. 2). Anyone who holds a position of authority is "God's servant," called to do God's will. The function of such an office is not to oppress the people, but to do them "good." Yet in order to maintain order, the office holder is granted special powers to punish wrongdoers, and is authorized to levy a tax (vv. 4–7).

25. The offices of human authority are instituted by God. But human *officeholders* may violate their office by acts of oppression that are contrary to God's intentions for maintaining an orderly society. Some societies make evangelism illegal; yet, in the Great Commission, Christ calls the Church to spread the Gospel. As in the Early Church, so in

China, Saudi Arabia, the Sudan, and Indonesia, Christians are called to obey God rather than men. The cost can be high, as anyone can discover by reading the magazine, *The Voice of the Martyrs*. Although we Christians must increasingly endure the scorn of secularists in the media and the academy, we can be thankful that in America we are not imprisoned, tortured, or killed for our faith.

26. Christians can show a Christlike submission to authority and love for others even in unfair and oppressive vocations, such as slavery. Paul explains that the slave is certainly entitled to try to gain his freedom by legal means (1 Corinthians 7:21) and discourages anyone from allowing themselves to be a slave (v. 23; see also Philemon verses 15–16). But the Christian is not justified in using violence to escape and, if there is no legal recourse, should see slavery as a means of Christlike service and witness (Ephesians 6:6).

Family Matters (Connect)

27. Paul notes that the Fourth commandment, "Honor your father and your mother," is the first one connected with a promise. The honoring of parents is connected to a good life here on earth, which is clearly impossible without an orderly society. Paul is saying that reverence for parental authority is necessary for a peaceful civil society. In his commentary on the Fourth Commandment in the Large Catechism, Luther explains that "honor" goes beyond the love we are enjoined to show to our neighbor. We are called to revere our parents as God's primary human representatives of God on earth. The Christian family is a small society, with parents as its rulers. It is a small church in which the earthly father models Christ, and his wife, the Church (Ephesians 5:24–25). In this way, the family is the primary building block for both civil society and the Church. It plays a foundational role in building both the earthly and heavenly kingdoms. This shows that defending and supporting family is not merely a fashionable political agenda; it is crucial to God's governance of humanity and calls for the commitment of all Christians.

28. Families frequently act as a unit. Just as a family is bound together by biological similarities, God calls whole families to be bound to Christ, the head of the body of Christ. When the jailor is converted, he knows his Christian duty to baptize his whole family, thereby putting their old selves to death and calling forth new life in Christ. This practice of family conversion is still common in Africa today, but modern individualism sometimes undermines it in the West.

Church and State (Vision)

29. Jesus explains that the kingdom of grace is not of this world. Our salvation does not depend on who has the most power here on earth, and the Church cannot win souls by the use of force (John 18:36). Force belongs to the earthly kingdom, and it is our government that has been authorized to bear the sword (Romans 13:4). But the sword can never change a person's heart or make them believe in Christ. Only the Holy Spirit can do this through the Gospel and the Sacraments. On the other hand, arrogant leaders are wrong in supposing that their authority is self-made. The power they do have to maintain order is always from above (John 19:11). But this power cannot save. We should obey our earthly leaders, but never entrust our souls to them (Psalm 146:3). Totalitarian regimes frequently require exclusive allegiance to the State, as if it is our Savior. But our salvation is found only in Christ, whose means of grace are offered by the Church and not the State. Discuss practical ways in which the role of Church and State can be confused. Do some Christians use force in inappropriate ways? Does the State trespass on the Gospel? Consider countries with state churches where ministers can be charged with breaking the law if they explain that God's Law opposes homosexuality or same-sex marriage.

30. Jesus does not call us out of the world into a separate, holy life. Nor does he call us to be worldly and conform our thoughts to worldly patterns of thinking (Romans 12:2). Instead, Jesus calls us to be in the world, but not of it (John 17:15–16). This is made possible by the "renewal of our mind" (Romans 12:2), a mind enabled to see God's will. Our vocation is where all of this happens. We are not asked to do amazing signs or to attain an elevated state of enlightenment, but to show Christ's love by forgetting ourselves and serving our neighbor right where we are. Discuss temptations to hide from the world or to become too worldly. Consider how Christ came into this world, pursuing His vocations, yet not resorting to worldly means of power and self-promotion. We can truthfully say that Christ fulfilled His vocations for us.

Ordered by Design

Objectives

By the power of the Holy Spirit working through God's Word, participants will (1) see that our God is a God of order, who has a harmonious design for human beings, (2) understand that men and women do not have identical vocations, and (3) realize that vocational boundaries are necessary to maintain order in society and the Church.

Opening Worship

Opening worship could begin with the commentary on the First Article of the Creed in the Small Catechism (*LSB* 322; *LW*, p. 301). Psalm 8 can be used as a prayer giving thanks for God's order for creation. An apt hymn is "Praise to the Lord, the Almighty" (*LSB* 790; *LW* 444).

Focus

31. Read, or ask a participant to read, the opening two paragraphs. Discuss why people resist the idea of order, structure, and hierarchy. Secularists often reject the special status God gives to humanity by claiming that we are no different than other animals. Some feminists reject the distinctive offices of wife and mother, appearing to resent the fact that God made men and women different. Statists would prefer that the State was our parent and that the "traditional family" withers away, as it is beginning to do in Scandinavia. But order is part of God's providential design for His creation and is necessary for harmonious living. Selfish, self-important people hurt others because they are not willing to entrust them with anything "important." We have all suffered the kitchen with too many cooks. All of God's work is important and needs to be done. We are called to follow God's design for our lives and use the gifts we have rather than trying to be something we are not, or to do something we are not called to do.

Made to Order (Inform)

God made human beings different from other creatures because He had special work for them to do. Likewise, He made women different from men and assigns distinctive roles to husband and wife, father and mother. Distinctions in God's design reflect God's desire for harmonious order, where each element in creation minds its own business and contributes to the functioning of the whole.

32. God is the Supreme Creator, who created all things out of nothing, and He created male and female in His image. He calls humans to be sub-creators, and gives them the responsibility of governing natural resources. We are called to do this through procreation and exercising the vocation of steward. Although God is the landlord who owns everything (Psalm 24:1) we are His stewards (Psalm 8:6), entrusted with the management of the natural world.

33. The first man was made *good* as was all of creation. Although he was good after his own kind, the man was made incomplete. Human beings are relational, social beings, and although Adam had a perfect relation with God, he did not have a social relation with another human being. For this reason, God says "It is not good that the man should be alone; I will make him a helper fit for him" (Genesis 2:18). We see that woman is created to help man and to complete him in a one-flesh union (v. 24). Woman is not created in the same way as man (vv. 22–23) and she is not assigned a completely independent role, just as the man is not completely independent of the woman. It is clear that Adam can only be completed by someone like him (human) yet different from him (designed and made differently). Adam would not have been completed by another man. The difference between man and woman therefore traces to an original difference in design, and is not merely a consequence of the conflict brought into the world by the fall.

34. Through Eve, the curse brings pains in childbearing and, just as humans were tempted to be like gods, the woman will desire to be like the man and to usurp his role as head of the woman (Genesis 3:16). This verse is sometimes misread by feminists as claiming that male headship is only a consequence of the fall, and that our renewal in Christ removes this distinction. As we saw, however, the distinction between man and woman is part of the original design of God. Through Adam, the curse brings pain and effort in our vocations, and it brings sickness, weakness, and death. But in verse 15 we see the first promise of a Messiah, who will save us from the consequences of sin by suffering and dying for our sins.

35. As Adam brought condemnation and death into the world, Christ brought justification and eternal life. Christ justifies by the great exchange. Christ took all of our sin upon Himself on the cross and atoned for it. In exchange, He then makes us righteous by giving us His own perfect righteousness. This righteousness is offered freely; it is not something we have earned. We are declared righteous because God accepted Christ's payment on our behalf, not because we have erased our debt. As a result, although we were "dead in our trespasses," God "made us alive together with Christ" (Ephesians 2:5). With this new life, we are thoroughly restored and re-equipped, "created in Christ Jesus for good works" (v. 10) out of gratitude for His salvation.

36. Marriage is patterned on and expresses (in the case of believers) the relationship of Christ and His Church. Believers are called to submit "to one another out of reverence for Christ" (Ephesians 5:21). Man and woman form a completed whole, a one-flesh marriage under the lordship of Christ. In marriage, submitting to one another here means that both man and woman accept the role appointed to them by God's design. But, as we saw, God did not design man and woman in the same way. Wives are called to submit to their husbands in the same way that the Church submits to Christ (vv. 22–24) and to "respect" their husbands (v. 33). Since the man represents Christ, he must love his wife in the same way as Christ loves the Church. The man is called to self-sacrificial love, to be a servant leader, who puts his wife's interests ahead of his own. The husband who loves his wife like his own body will look after and care for his wife (vv. 28–29), in sickness and in health, until death.

Order in Society (Connect)

37. When people reject external authority, they become their own authority. Each person becomes his own king. But people have different desires and interests, and so the many self-appointed kings, each of whom rejects the authority of all the others, make conflict inevitable. There will be constant battles for power, wealth, and prestige. In his second letter to Timothy, Paul tells us that, in the last days, there will be an increase of narcissism, greed for money, rudeness and disobedience, ingratitude, an inability to forgive, slander, brutality, false piety, Machiavellian scheming, and suppression of the truth.

Contemporary examples will vary. Disrespect for teachers, the police, political leaders, and the clergy are obvious cases.

38. Just as in Paul's time, Christians are called to give up the selfish desires that cause disorder and disrespect for God's design for family and society. We must eschew uncontrolled sensuality (1 Peter 4:2–4), but

remain "self-controlled and sober-minded" (v. 7) so that we can pray and show love and hospitality to others (vv. 8–9). The gifts we have are entrusted to us so that we may use them to faithfully serve others (v. 10). When we do this, we contribute to maintaining an orderly community.

Specific examples of gifts and opportunities to serve today will vary. Emphasize that Christians should be the *doctors* for their society, diagnosing its ills and offering remedies.

Order in the Church (Vision)

39. Since our God is a God of order, it is important that we observe order in the Church. In worship, each contribution should help build up the Church (1 Corinthians 14:26). Liturgy has been devised so that we understand the proper relation between God and man. We invoke God's name to show our submission to His authority. We confess our sins, and hear the words of Absolution from a pastor who stands in the place of Christ Himself. We respond with songs of praise. We must remember that the Church is not focused on us and our words, but on God's Word for our life. The Word of God did not originate with us. Cutesy self-help sermons and people-centered hymns teach the false doctrine that we save ourselves by getting ourselves right with God or by improving our lives.

40. We also show respect for God's design by understanding that He has distinctive work for women in the church. As men are called to represent Christ in the context of marriage, they are also called to represent Christ in the Church. Women are every bit as valuable and important to God as men, but women are not called to be pastors. We must remember that God exalts the humble and humiliates the proud. Mary is granted a gift, given to no man, of being the very mother of God. It is women, not men, who first bring the news of the risen Christ. Mary's *Magnificat* (Luke 1:46–55) provides a wonderful model for women's vocations in the Church.

The Great Dance

Objectives

By the power of the Holy Spirit working through God's Word, participants will (1) understand why God has many different "parts" for people to play, (2) see that each person has many vocations, but all are connected, and (3) realize that God may change our vocations, sometimes through unpleasant circumstances.

Opening Worship

Opening worship could begin by reading together the Apostles' Creed and noting the distinct work of the three persons of our triune God. A fitting prayer would be the Collect for The Holy Trinity (*LSB Altar Book*, p. 906; *LW*, p. 61). An apt hymn would be "Father Most Holy" (*LSB* 504; *LW* 175), any trinitarian hymn, or the *Te Deum*.

Focus

41. Read, or have a participant read, the opening paragraphs. Answers will vary. Proud people do not trust other people to do a good job and take on all the work by themselves. The contributions of others are ignored, causing hard feelings. The results are often poor. The soccer player who will not pass when he should is usually tackled, so the whole team loses an opportunity to score. When each player thinks of his work as a contribution to the team's objective, the team functions effectively. Vocations are to be understood not as isolated walks of life but as contributions to a collaborative project.

A Play with Many Parts (Inform)

Vocations exist in interdependence. One actor says his line to set up the next actor for her line. Otherwise we have one character taking everyone's part and doing a monologue. This ignores the gifts that other actors have been given, and rejects the author's intention for the play. Recognizing vocation is recognizing our particular contribution to a community project that also involves the vocations of others. It rejects an "I can do it all" or "I did it my way" approach. Frank Sinatra's song fails to capture the fact that human beings flourish in community, not by self-assertion, but by a combination of humble service and dependence on the gifts of others.

42. Repenting of our sin is not repenting of our existence in the world. God created the world good. Even after the fall, He expects Christians to remain in their various stations where they can best show His love to their neighbor. John does tell tax collectors and soldiers to conduct their work ethically, but he does not tell them to resign. This reflects the fact that both taxation and the military are part of the human government that God institutes to maintain order on earth. And it also shows that every vocation is under God's Law. Tax collectors and soldiers who extort money or make false accusations are acting outside of their vocation.

43. There are so many different vocations because God has assigned different functions and distributed different gifts to different people. Just as the various parts of the body have different functions but each contributes to the life of the body, so there are different callings that together support the life of a community.

44. It is easy to suppose that eyes are more important than hands because we need eyes to see where we are going. Likewise, political leaders may be tempted to think they are more important than workers. But what use is it to see the steering wheel if one has no hands to control it? And what government could survive in a world without farmers and factory workers? Yet those workers also need political leaders so that society is well run and taxes are collected for education, services, and the military. Otherwise the workers are not trained, have no infrastructure to get to work, and are vulnerable to attack. The fact is that each vocation is dependent on the others. Each vocation is crucial to the healthy functioning of the civil community and of the body of Christ.

45. In order for the great dance of community to work, each Christian must be self-controlled (1 Thessalonians 4:4–5), should avoid wronging or taking advantage of his brother or sister (v. 6), and should love others (vv. 9–10). This love is shown in part through obedience to vocation, accepting the assigned role that God has given us. In verse 11, Christians are called to "live quietly" (avoiding conflict and discord), to mind their "own affairs" (focusing on serving their neighbor through their own vocation and not trespassing on the vocations of others), and to work with their "hands" (actually do the work themselves and not make others do it for them). All of this is done to create a harmonious working community so that the daily lives of Christians "may live properly before

outsiders" (v. 12) by serving as a collective witness to Christ through a life of cooperative self-sacrifice.

46. Vocations are not our choices, but God's choices for us. When we abdicate vocation, it is like an organ of our body shutting down. The whole body suffers because a function critical to the whole is not being performed. Those who neglect their talents let down not only themselves but the whole community, which is justified in imposing punishment on the idler (2 Thessalonians 3:10). Paul argues that the person who refuses to use his gifts to support the whole cannot expect support from others until he repents and makes his contribution.

47. Hard workers are busy pursuing their assigned vocation. A busybody ignores his own vocation and interferes with everyone else's because he is so sure he can do it better. A good way to annoy people is to appoint oneself a supervisor who constantly critiques everyone else's work while doing absolutely none of one's own. Paul says that such people are called to return to their own vocation and to "earn their own living" (2 Thessalonians 3:12) like everyone else. Vocation opposes self-importance and self-appointed, self-made people, and exalts those who allow God to make of them a servant for the whole.

Wearing Many Hats (Connect)

48. Anyone who serves as an overseer (or bishop or pastor) will at the same time be a monogamous husband, a teacher (1 Timothy 3:2), a parent (v. 4), and a longtime Christian (v. 6). He makes it clear that overseers and deacons must pursue their other vocations in ways compatible with their vocation as a minister.

Contemporary examples of holding multiple vocations will vary. It is important to see that a Christian businessman and parent is called to conduct business and raise his children in ways that reflect his primary call to be a Christian. A crooked businessman, wife-beater, or child abuser who worships regularly is not a good witness, or a faithful servant, despite his outward but false piety.

49. Every vocation is an opportunity for witness. Paul uses his vocation as teacher of the Jewish Law to defend the Gospel "against all the accusations of the Jews" (Acts 26:2) by arguing that Jesus fulfills the promises given to the twelve tribes of Israel (v. 7). Using his expertise in Greek philosophy, Paul also witnesses to the Gentiles (v. 20) and as a lawyer provides public evidence to support his case for Christ (v. 26). Finally, he uses his vocation as Roman citizen so that he can appeal to Caesar (v. 32) and witness in Rome.

Contemporary examples will vary. The main point is that we have opportunities to witness as spouse, parent, worker, citizen, and member of a congregation. Each vocation is a distinctive avenue for witness. By pursuing that vocation in a Christlike manner, we embody the Gospel for those with whom the vocation connects us.

A Road Less Traveled (Vision)

50. Joseph's brothers sold Joseph into slavery, wresting him away from his vocations at home. But God drew Joseph to a new calling: he is put in charge of the "all the land of Egypt" (Genesis 41:41), where he exercises wise stewardship by storing grain from the abundant years so that famine could be endured. Although Joseph's brothers had meant to harm Joseph, God used their evil actions to work good for Israel. Joseph's new vocation enables him to do God's providential work by saving Israel from starvation.

Contemporary examples will vary. Even if we suffer hardships such as job loss, illness, or divorce, which tear us away from our current vocations, God will provide new work for us to do. A painful experience may lead to a new opportunity to serve.

51. We can be mistaken in supposing something is not our calling when it is. Moses thought he had no gift to lead Israel because he was not a confident speaker. But God made Moses the leader, saying what God commanded and working through the medium of Aaron (Exodus 7:1–2). Paul thought his goal in life was to round up Christian "blasphemers" for extradition, but he was chosen by God to carry His name "before the Gentiles and kings and the children of Israel" (Acts 9:15).

Contemporary examples will vary. Teachers are often required to teach in areas outside their original training. In the business world, retraining and reassignment is common. Pastors are called to different congregations, to mission work, or to become theology faculty.

God at Work

Objectives

By the power of the Holy Spirit working through God's Word, participants will (1) understand that our God works through us for the benefit of our neighbor, (2) see how we all depend upon each other's vocation, and (3) give credit to God alone for any good works we do, for He is the source of all the love and gifts that motivate us.

Opening Worship

Worship could begin with a responsive reading of Psalm 147, which emphasizes God's ongoing work in creation, including humanity. An appropriate prayer is the Collect of the Day for the First Sunday after the Epiphany (*LSB Altar Book*, One-Year Lectionary, p. 854) or the Fifth Sunday after the Epiphany (*LW*, p. 26). An apt hymn is "'Come Follow Me' Said Christ the Lord" (*LW* 379).

Focus

52. Read, or have a participant read, the first two paragraphs. Answers will vary. Everyone runs into unexpected demands. Someone else needs heavy lifting, dishes to pass, or repairs on the house. Sometimes we can help, sometimes we cannot, and sometimes we are the ones that need help. God works through people where they are and with the gifts that He has given them. Ability and opportunity suffice to make the call to serve. This is often unexpected, and sometimes we are unwilling to help. God prefers a willing helper who forgets himself or herself, but He will still work through an unwilling helper, changing him or her as He does so. I am sometimes reluctant to put up the Christmas tree, but I am always glad when I have done it.

Our Servant God (Inform)

God serves us in order to call forth our service to others. But God does not merely tell us to serve. Through faith, the Gospel changes us, so that we find a new desire to serve. God does this by working through us, by uniting us with Christ and giving us the love of Christ.

53. God is concerned for our temporal needs of food, drink, and clothing. He provides the raw materials for all of this in our natural environment and calls human beings to create the products. But He wants us to remember that salvation is not found here. God's providence for this life must always be held secondary to the gift of eternal life. Our vocations are important to serve our neighbor, but God ultimately calls us home to live with Him.

54. Jesus humbled Himself to wash His disciples' feet (John 13:14) so that we would see our calling to forget our pride and serve others in humility. A Christian should not be like the butler who "doesn't do floors." Even a Christian CEO may be called to help a disabled person rake leaves or shovel snow. Those who humble themselves to meet the real needs of others are exalted by God as heroes of the faith, even if the world takes no notice. What matters is the love and the witness given to the person who is helped.

55. God works through us by filling us "with the knowledge of His will in all spiritual wisdom and understanding" (Colossians 1:9). This spiritual discernment enables us to see our vocation. We are also provided with power to bear "fruit in every good work" (v. 10) and receive gifts of endurance, patience, and joyful gratitude for being made heirs of Christ's inheritance (vv. 11–13). Paul tells us that the fruit of the Spirit includes "love, joy, peace, patience, kindness, goodness, faithfulness, gentleness, [and] self-control" (Galatians 5:22).

56. Paul addresses factions in the church of Corinth that arise from disagreements about who is the best human leader. These disagreements show a failure to understand that human beings are servants and conduits of God's saving grace (1 Corinthians 3:5). None of us has any power to save in ourselves: "neither he who plants nor he who waters is anything, but only God who gives the growth" (v. 7). Thus we are "God's fellow workers" (v. 9) in the same sense that tenant farmers are fellow workers with the landowner. The landowner works through the tenants to produce crops, but the land and the crops are his. Although all vocations are opportunities for evangelism, we never save anyone. God saves by the power of the Holy Spirit working through the Gospel. Likewise, although all vocations are opportunities to show love to our neighbor, it is God's love that is being shown through us.

57. Notice first that God can even work through insincere people (Philippians 1:18). Even if the Gospel is preached insincerely, the Holy Spirit can still work through the Word. More generally, God is at work in humans even when they do not cooperate. Also note that although Paul

would like to be with the Lord in heaven, he recognizes that God has work for him to do here on earth (vv. 24–25). Like the captain of a ship, we are not authorized to abandon our station when we feel like it.

58. We are to Christ as the branches are to the vine. We have no spiritual life of our own, no natural ability to bear fruit (John 15:4), but, if we are connected to Christ, we will bear abundant fruit (v. 5). Paul explores several similar analogies. He says we are no longer aliens but "fellow citizens," no longer outcasts but "members of the household of God" (Ephesians 2:19). And we are stones of a building raised "on the foundation of the apostles and prophets" (God's Word) with "Christ Jesus Himself being the cornerstone" (v. 20). The common bond of each stone in the building is its incorporation in Christ and submission to God's Word. The Holy Spirit also is a tie that binds us together into God's dwelling place (v. 22).

Mutual Dependence (Connect)

59. God made us social beings. We are designed for relationship, to work together. Our gifts are not provided to exalt ourselves in isolation from others but are means of playing our part in a wider community. Everyone needs the support of others with different gifts. Many people cannot fix their own plumbing or electrics and do not know how to put on a new roof or fix their car. God does not want "division in the body" (1 Corinthians 12:25) where some people view themselves as self-sufficient or superior, so he distributes His gifts in such a way that everyone depends on others. That helps us to see that we are in this together, that the suffering and honor of some impacts everyone (v. 26). God creates this mutual dependence "for building up the body of Christ, until we all attain to the unity of the faith and of the knowledge of the Son of God" (Ephesians 4:12–13). As each part does its work, Christians abandon deception by "speaking the truth in love," and the body of Christ grows up into the Head, Christ (vv. 15–16).

Contemporary examples of the failure of individualism may vary.

60. Each of us has assigned vocations, a burden we are called to carry. But our vocations are not unrelated to other people's. As we bear our own load (Galatians 6:5) by following our vocation, we must also "bear one another's burdens" (v. 2) by supporting other people's vocations. For example, a builder is called to build, but his work will fail if the architect's blueprint is faulty or if the contractors do not deliver the materials on time. Likewise, the architect is called to design the house to be structurally sound, but his plans are not realized if the builder deviates from the plan or if the contractors deliver defective materials. We always

have a twofold responsibility to complete the work assigned to us, and to make sure that it serves those other workers who depend on it.

Contemporary illustrations may vary.

Consider the Source (Vision)

61. John explains that all true, unconditional (*agape*) love comes from God. Anyone capable of showing this divine love "has been born of God" (has been regenerated) and "knows God" (1 John 4:7). In Christ, God came into the world so that we see His love and share in that love by living through Christ (v. 9). By ourselves, we cannot love God, but God's love empowers us to love others (vv. 11–12). It is not possible to live in God's love without loving our neighbor (vv. 20–21). The good Samaritan is both Christ Himself, sacrificing Himself to save helpless humanity, and the Christian, who is called to do likewise by sacrificing his own interests to serve his neighbor.

Contemporary applications may vary. We cannot claim to show the love of God if we are unloving to the poor, other races, the divorced, homosexuals, or drug addicts.

62. James reminds us that every "good gift and every perfect gift is from above" (James 1:17). God gave us a new birth through the Gospel (v. 18). This creates a free heartfelt desire to help. We can trust that "he who supplies seed to the sower and bread for food will" also supply our hearts with spiritual seeds that produce a "harvest of . . . righteousness" (2 Corinthians 9:10). Our generous Father enriches us so that we may be generous to others (v. 11). God values generosity because it reflects gratitude to God (v. 12) and because it causes men to "glorify God because of your submission flowing from your confession of the gospel of Christ" (v. 13).

Contemporary applications will vary. Churches witness most effectively when they combine evangelism with a concern for the temporal needs of others. Food pantries, parish nurse programs, and church schools are a few among many examples.

Appendix of Lutheran Teaching

Below you will find examples of how the first Lutherans addressed the issue of vocation. They will help you understand the Lutheran difference.

Vocation in the Lutheran Confessions

Vocation intersects with every major theological doctrine. God calls human beings into vocations by creating them for special work. He brings hardship to these vocations by the curse of the fall. But vocations continue as channels of God's providential love of His creation. Non-Christians are compelled to serve so that social order is maintained. But Christians are reborn in Christ to a new willingness to serve their neighbor and spread the Gospel. Finally, Christ calls believers out of this world into life eternal with Him.

The Augsburg Confession

Article II: Original Sin (1–2)

Our churches teach that since the fall of Adam (Romans 5:12), all who are naturally born are born with sin (Psalm 51:5), that is, without the fear of God, without trust in God, and with the inclination to sin, called concupiscence. Concupiscence is a disease and original vice that is truly sin. It damns and brings eternal death on those who are not born anew through Baptism and the Holy Spirit (John 3:5).

Article VI: New Obedience (1–2)

Our churches teach that this faith is bound to bring forth good fruit (Galatians 5:22–23). It is necessary to do good works commanded by God (Ephesians 2:10), because of God's will. We should not rely on those works to merit justification before God. The forgiveness of sins and justification is received through faith.

Article XIV: Order in the Church

Our churches teach that no one should publicly teach in the Church, or administer the Sacraments, without a rightly ordered call.

Article XVI: Civil Government (1–2)

Our churches teach that lawful civil regulations are good works of God. They teach that it is right for Christians to hold political office, to serve as judges, to judge matters by imperial laws and other existing laws, to impose just punishments, to engage in just wars, to serve as soldiers, to make legal contracts, to hold property, to take oaths when required by magistrates, for a man to marry a wife, or a woman to be given in marriage (Romans 13; 1 Corinthians 7:2).

Article XX: Good Works (9–10, 27–28)

First, [our teachers] teach that our works cannot reconcile God to us or merit forgiveness of sins, grace, and justification. We obtain reconciliation only by faith when we believe that we are received into favor for Christ's sake. He alone has been set forth as the Mediator and Atoning Sacrifice (1 Timothy 2:5), in order that the Father may be reconciled through Him. Therefore, whoever believes that he merits grace by works despises the merit and grace of Christ (Galatians 5:4). . . . We teach that it is necessary to do good works. This does not mean that we merit grace by doing good works, but because it is God's will (Ephesians 2:10). It is only by faith, and nothing else, that forgiveness of sins is apprehended. The Holy Spirit is received through faith, hearts are renewed and given new affections, and then they are able to bring forth good works.

Luther's Small Catechism

The Apostles' Creed: First Article and Explanation

I believe in God, the Father Almighty, maker of heaven and earth. *What does this mean?* Answer: I believe that God has made me and all creatures. He has given me my body and soul, eyes, ears, and all my limbs, my reason, and all my senses, and still preserves them. In addition, He has given me clothing and shoes, meat and drink, house and home, wife and children, fields, cattle, and all my goods. He provides me richly and daily with all that I need to support this body and life. He protects me from all danger and guards me and preserves me from all evil. He does all this out of pure, fatherly, divine goodness and mercy, without any merit or worthiness in me. For all this I ought to thank Him, praise Him, serve Him, and obey Him. This is most certainly true.

Second Article and Explanation

And in Jesus Christ, His only Son, our Lord, who was conceived by the Holy Spirit, born of the Virgin Mary, suffered under Pontius Pilate, was crucified, died and was buried. He descended into hell. The third day He rose again from the dead. He ascended into heaven and sits at the right hand of God the Father Almighty. From thence He will come to judge the living and the dead. *What does this mean?* Answer: I believe that Jesus Christ, true God, begotten of the Father from eternity, and also true man, born of the Virgin Mary, is my Lord. He has redeemed me, a lost and condemned creature, purchased and won me from all sins, from death, and from the power of the devil. He did this not with gold or silver, but with His holy, precious blood and with His innocent suffering and death, so that I may be His own, live under Him in His kingdom, and serve Him in everlasting righteousness, innocence, and blessedness, just as He is risen from the dead, lives and reigns to all eternity. This is most certainly true.

Third Article and Explanation

I believe in the Holy Spirit, the holy Christian Church, the communion of saints, the forgiveness of sins, the resurrection of the body, and the life everlasting. Amen. *What does this mean?* Answer: I believe that I cannot by my own reason or strength believe in Jesus Christ, my Lord, or come to Him. But the Holy Spirit has called me by the Gospel, enlightened me with His gifts, sanctified and kept me in the true faith. In the same way He calls, gathers, enlightens, and sanctifies the whole Christian Church on earth and keeps it with Jesus Christ in the one true faith. In this Christian Church He daily and richly forgives all my sins and the sins of all believers. On the Last Day He will raise up me and all the dead and will give eternal life to me and to all believers in Christ. This is most certainly true.

Glossary

Baptism. Through water joined to God's Word, the Holy Spirit puts to death our sinful nature, connects us to Christ in His death and resurrection, and gives us new spiritual birth as God's children.
first (civil) use of the Law. The Law is a curb to restrain sin and disorder designed to allow life in community to continue.
God's image (*imago Dei*). In Lutheran teaching, the image of God is man's original righteousness that he possessed in the garden before the fall. This image was lost through sin (Romans 1:23). While after the fall man possesses rationality, creativity, and the like, and although these are sometimes referred to as "vestiges," "remnants," or "traces" of the image of God, these concreated gifts are not possessed in a state of perfection as they were before the fall. Without original righteousness, these gifts are not properly called "the image of God." Yet by the Holy Spirit, who works through the Gospel in Word and Sacraments, the image of God is being restored in believers as they are being conformed to the image of Christ (Romans 8:29; 2 Corinthians 3:18; Colossians 3:10).
good works. God's love works through us to serve our neighbor. In faith, we cooperate with God's gracious will to care for him or her.
Gospel. The message of Christ's death and resurrection for the forgiveness of sins and eternal life. The Holy Spirit works through the Gospel to create and sustain faith and to empower good works. The Gospel is found in both the Old and New Testaments.
grace. Properly, God's good will and favor in and through Jesus Christ, toward sinners, who can plead no merit or worthiness. Scripture also refers to grace in the sense of a gift God gives to people.
justification. God declares sinners to be just or righteous for Christ's sake; that is, God has imputed or charged our sins to Christ, and He imputes or credits Christ's righteousness to us.
Law. God's will that shows people how they should live (e.g., the Ten Commandments) and condemns their failure. The preaching of the Law is the cause of contrition, or genuine sorrow over sin. The Law is found in both the Old and New Testaments.

marriage. The publicly recognized, lifelong relationship of two opposite-sex individuals for the purpose of mutual support, sexual intimacy, and the bearing and nurture of children. Jesus affirmed the biblical basis for traditional marriage, the lifelong one-flesh union of husband and wife (Matthew 19:4–6).

neighbor. The person my circumstances and gifts call me to serve.

sanctification. The spiritual growth that follows justification by grace through faith in Christ. Sanctification is God's work through His means of grace: the Gospel and the Sacraments.

sinful nature. Our human nature, after the fall, is thoroughly corrupted by sin, making us God's enemies and lovers of ourselves.

two kingdoms. God's "left hand" kingdom governs temporal matters and all our dealings with others here on earth. God's "right hand" kingdom governs our hearts by His grace through faith in Christ.

vocation.

    as part of humanity's design. All humans are called to be stewards, although men and women are called to complementary roles of husband and wife, father and mother.

    as a call to the new person in Christ. The call to serve our neighbor freely, out of gratitude for Christ's salvation and without the compulsion of the Law.

    as a relationship manifest in God's own triune nature. The Father calls the Son to be obedient, and rewards His humiliation with exaltation. The Spirit is called to proceed from the Father and the Son to convict the world of sin and draw men to saving faith.

    as foundation of family. Husband and wife, mother and father, and children all have distinct vocations that bind the family unit together into a harmonious whole. The family is the basis for every other community including civil society and the Church.

    as foundation of the State (civil order). Vocations are contributions to the social order. Each vocation contributes to, and depends on, other vocations needed for society to function.

    as foundation of the Church (Christ's body). The pastor is called to stand in the place of Christ, calling the congregation to confession, announcing Absolution, proclaiming God's Word, and administering the Sacraments. Each member of the congregation is called by his or her distinctive gifts and opportunities to serve and make contributions that build up the body of Christ.